doodle jump®

where's doodle?

A Doodle Jump Search Book

SCHOLASTIC

The Adventures of Doodle

Doodle the Doodler is jumping all around the world! Your mission is to track him on his travels and see if you can spot him in each scene – as well as the friends he makes along the way. Don't lose sight of that Doodle Jumper!

this book belongs to _____

You'll find our hero hiding somewhere in every scene, so keep a sharp lookout for his jumping feet. Don't get distracted by his costumed cousins – the original Doodler will be lurking somewhere! Then check out the questions in the scroll bar and see what else you can spot.

have fun!

doodle jump is awesome because _____

I am ____ years old.

if I could jump anywhere in the world I'd go to _____

my top doodle jump score is _____

my best friend's top doodle jump score is ____

I live in _____

the coolest thing about Doodle is _____

doodle jump®
Dive In!

Doodle's first adventure lies at the bottom of the ocean. He's getting to know the weird and wonderful creatures of the deep. Can you track him down?

Be careful you don't get distracted by Doodle's deep-sea diving friends.

How many of these other strange undersea animals can you spot?

doodle jump®

Easter Egg-xercise

Doodle has stumbled across a giant Easter egg hunt. Can you find him without stopping to eat all the chocolate?

Don't get put off by his friends in Easter disguises.

How many of these crazy Easter extras can you spot?

9

doodle jump®
On Safari

Deep in the mighty jungle, something scary is stirring . . .

It's your job to save Doodle from the monsters of the unexplored wilderness, so hop onto the nearest elephant and start searching.

Don't be distracted by Doodle's safari friends. Jump to it!

How many of these jungle dwellers can you find?

doodle jump®

Perfect Pyramids

Doodle has travelled to Egypt, but some of the quirky creatures he's met so far are also on his trail. Can you be the first to find him?

How many of these other ancient Egyptian inhabitants can you spot?

doodle jump®
Behind You!

Daring Doodle has entered the land of the ninjas. Can you spot him skulking among the shadows?

How many of Doodle's nimble ninja friends can you find?

damsel
in distress!

zap!

Land of HEROES

Doodle's going to fit right in in this land, so he'll definitely be tricky to find. Keep searching and channel your inner hero.

How many of Doodle's other fearless friends can you spot?

17

doodle jump®

Doodle Planet Cup

Doodle's somewhere on the Doodle Planet Cup stadium pitch! Hunt for him quickly – but don't miss any goals!

How many of these football stars from around the world can you find?

doodle jump®

Pirates

Oo-arr, me hearties, Doodle's sailing the high seas with a band of wild pirates. Navigate your way towards him, but don't get caught or you might have to walk the plank!

How many of these putrid pirates can you find?

doodle jump®
Trick or Treat?

The sun has set and the moon is hidden behind ghostly clouds. Who is lurking under cover of darkness, waiting to pounce? Find Doodle before something unpleasant finds you!

How many of these creepy critters can you spot?

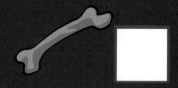

Crowding Round

Oh no! We've lost Doodle in the crowd. Can you seek him out before we lose him for good?

How many of these other crazy Doodle Jump characters can you spot?

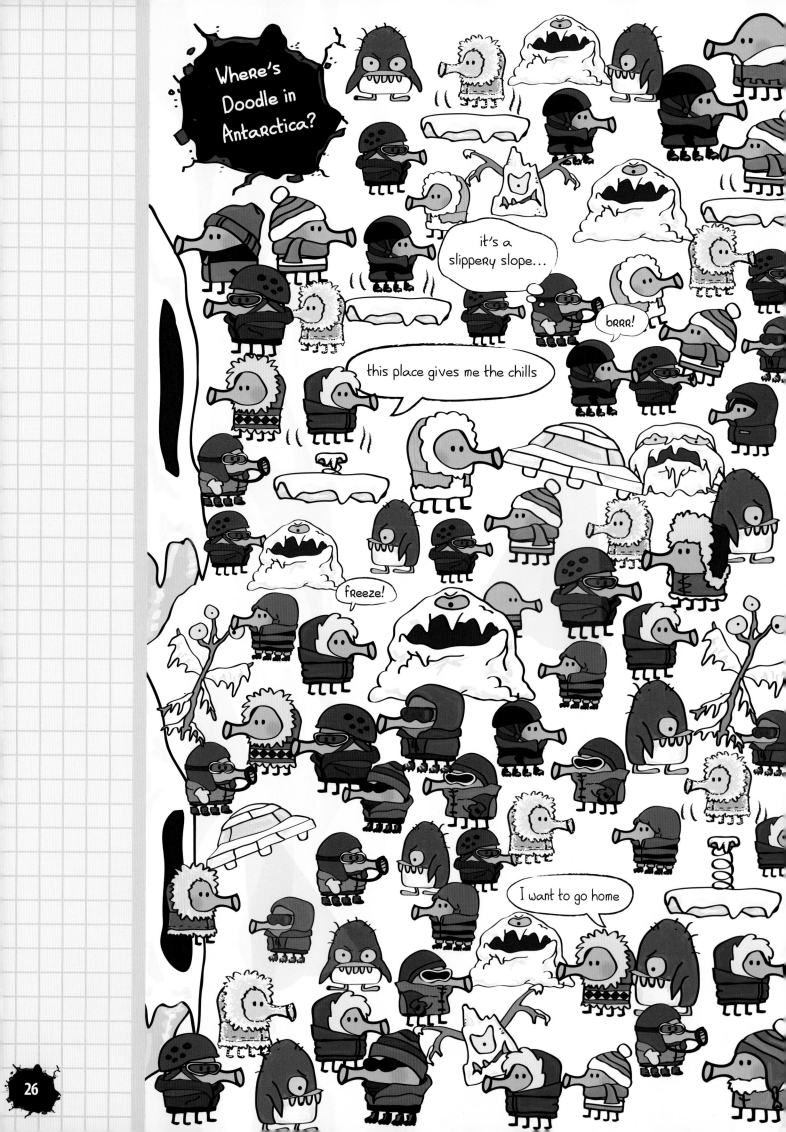

doodle jump®
Antarctic Adventure

Doodle has entered the frozen land of Antarctica. Follow him as he treks over glaciers and snowy mountains, and find his chilly hiding place! Brrr! He must be cold.

How many of these other icy explorers can you spot?

 ☐

 ☐

 ☐

 ☐

 ☐

Doctor, Doctor

Poor Doodle caught a cold on his icy adventure, so he needs a little first aid. Find him in the hospital – but watch out for some less fortunate patients wandering the halls!

How many other weird and wonderful hospital inhabitants can you spot?

doodle jump

On Your Marks...

Doodle's feeling the need for speed! Can you track him down before he runs into trouble?

How many of his rowdy racer friends and obstacles can you find?

doodle jump®
Land of Ancients

Ancient civilisations are smashed together in Doodle's next exciting destination. Can you find him among the kings, queens and warriors of long ago?

Can you also spot Doodle's historical cousins? How many of each can you find in this scene?

doodle jump
Blast Off!

Your mission is taking you up to the stars! Doodle has blasted into space and where he goes, you must follow. Can you find him among the planets, astronauts and alien life forms?

How many of these other space invaders can you spot?

doodle jump®

Merry Christmas

Phew! Doodle made it back to planet Earth in time for Christmas. He's brought a few aliens with him though! Get festive and unwrap your searching skills.

How many of these Christmas critters can you find?

doodle jump®
Party Time!

After all his travels, Doodle is finally home where he belongs, and he's brought back some of the creatures he met along the way. To celebrate, his friends have thrown him a massive fancy-dress party! But Doodle forgot his costume.

Can you spot him among all his dressed-up friends?

How many of these other party guests can you find?

39

Answers

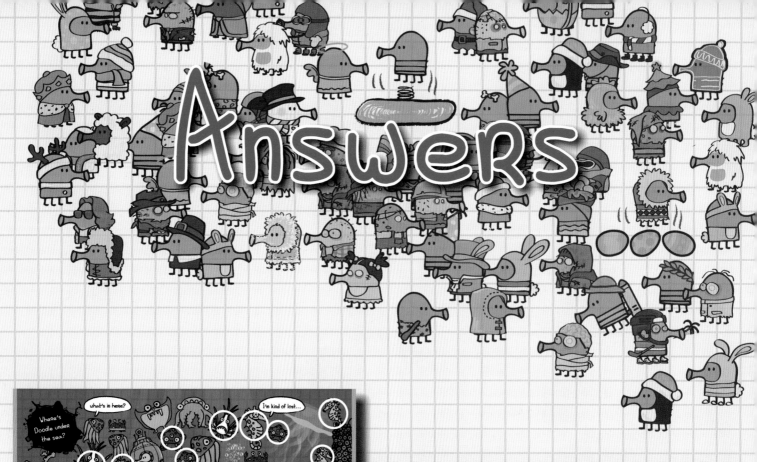

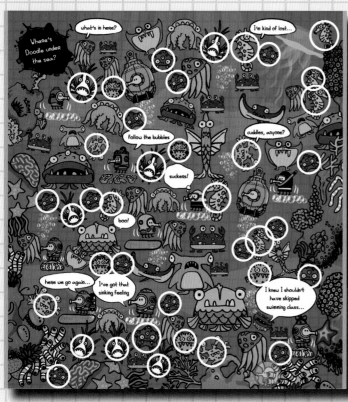

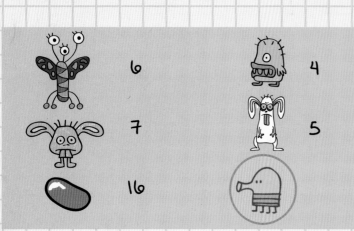

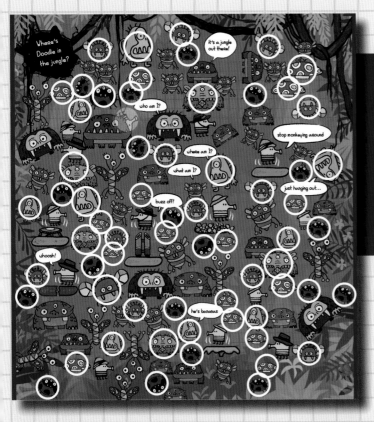

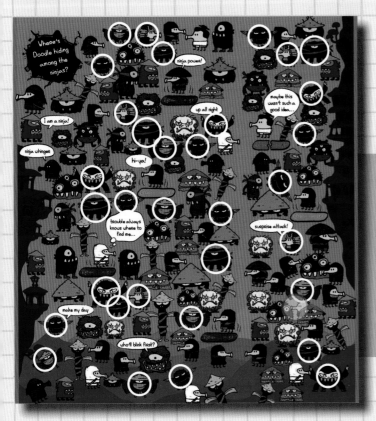

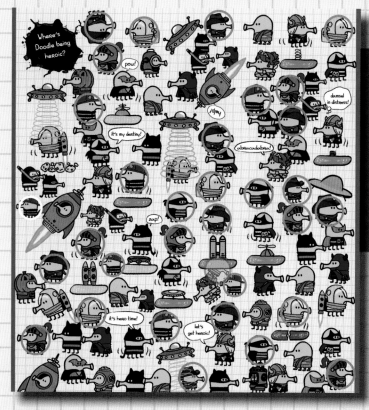

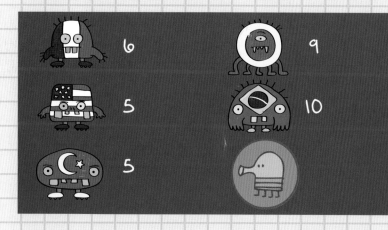

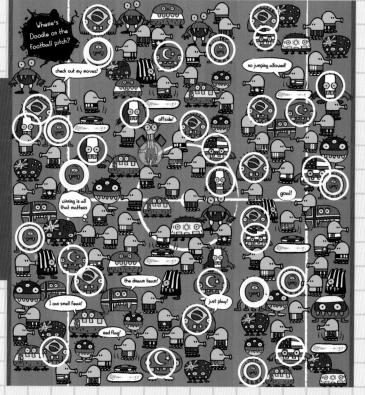

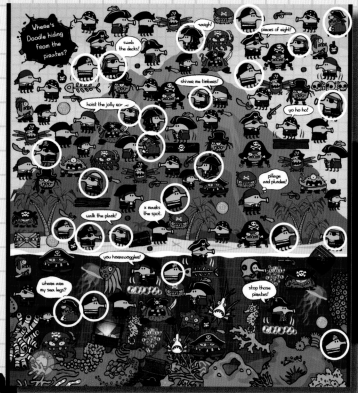

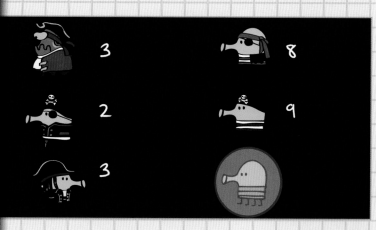

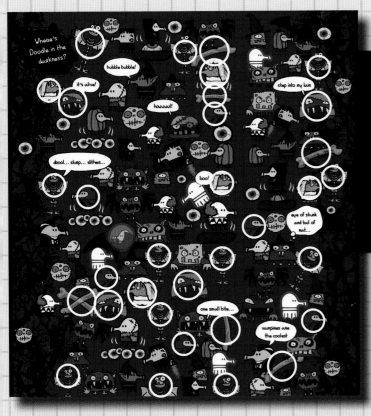

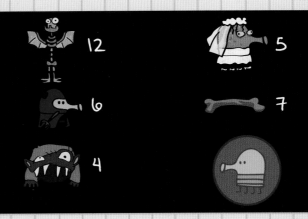

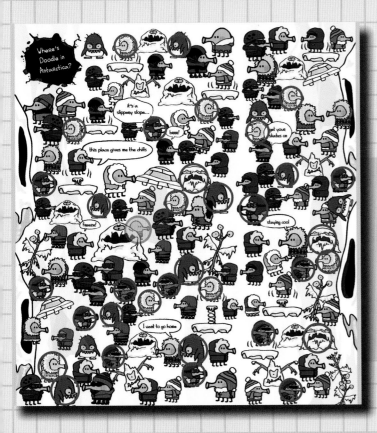

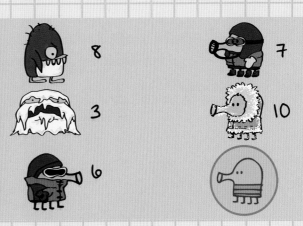

43

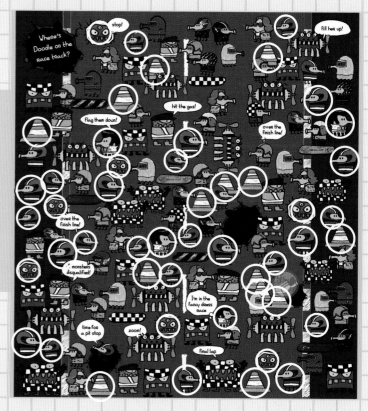

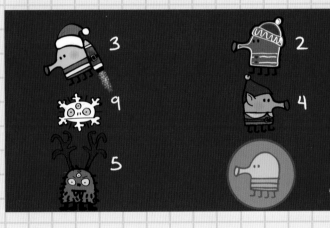

Produced under licence by
Scholastic Children's Books,
Euston House, 24 Eversholt Street,
London NW1 1DB, UK

© Lima Sky LLC, 2015

ISBN 978 1407 15634 7

Printed in Malaysia

2 4 6 8 10 9 7 5 3 1

www.scholastic.co.uk